The Civil War

Brother Against Brother

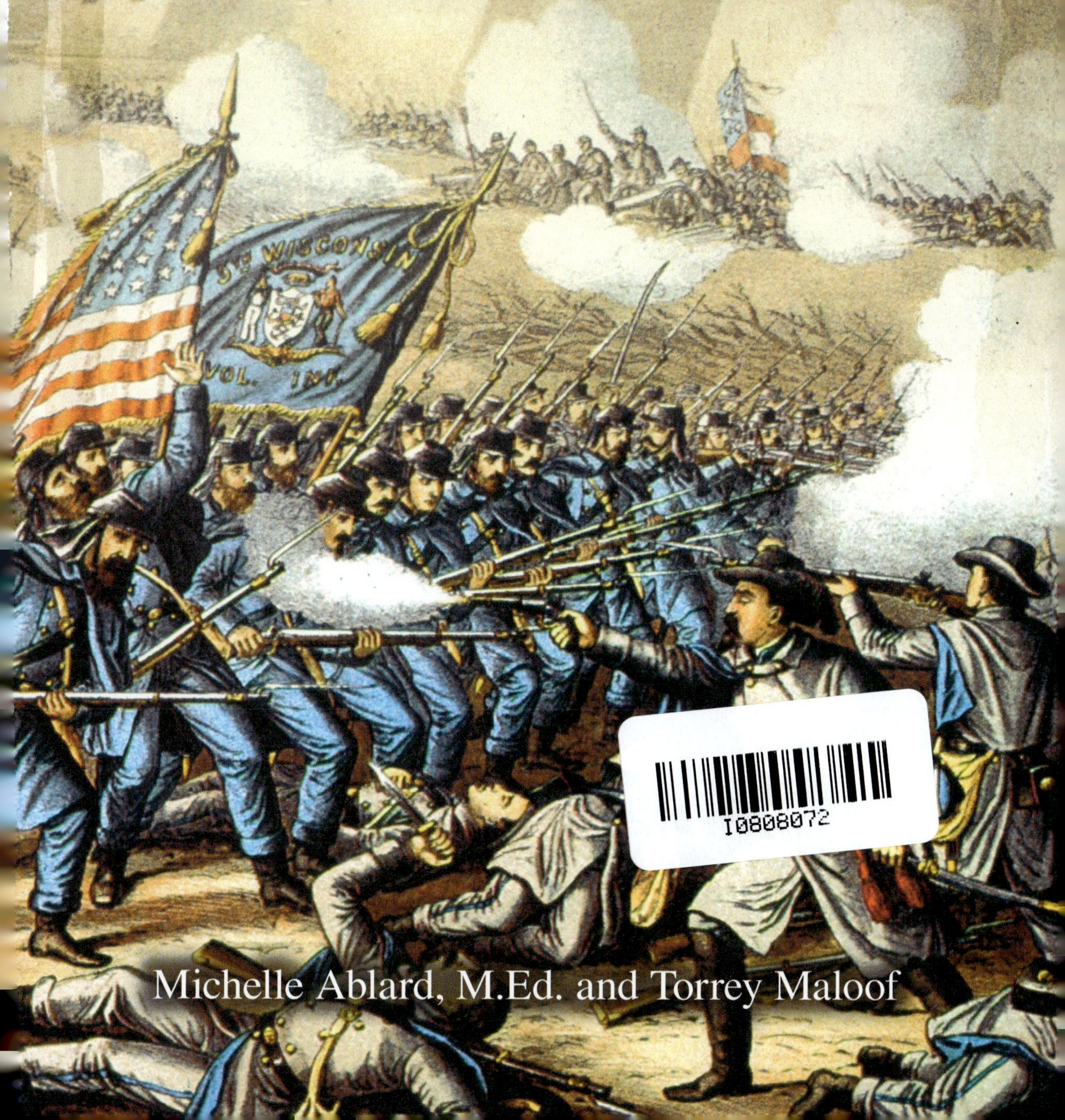

Michelle Ablard, M.Ed. and Torrey Maloof

Consultants

Vanessa Ann Gunther, Ph.D.
Department of History
Chapman University

Nicholas Baker, Ed.D.
Supervisor of Curriculum and Instruction
Colonial School District, DE

Katie Blomquist, Ed.S.
Fairfax County Public Schools

Publishing Credits

Rachelle Cracchiolo, M.S.Ed., *Publisher*
Conni Medina, M.A.Ed., *Managing Editor*
Emily R. Smith, M.A.Ed., *Series Developer*
Diana Kenney, M.A.Ed., NBCT, *Content Director*
Courtney Patterson, *Senior Graphic Designer*
Torrey Maloof, *Editor*

Image Credits: pp. 2, 11, 13 Sarin Images/Granger, NYC; pp. 4-5 Campbell Family Papers, 1860-1886. P 900150. South Carolina Department Archives and History, Columbia, South Carolina; p. 5 (bottom) Peter Newark Military Pictures/Bridgeman Images; pp. 6, 15 North Wind Picture Archives; p. 7 (bottom) LOC [LC-DIG-det-4a07284]; pp. 7, 11 (top and middle), 17 (top), 28 (right) Granger, NYC; p. 8 (top) LOC [LC-DIG-ppmsca-19238], (bottom) LOC [LC-USZ62-17728]; p. 9 LOC [ct000764]; p. 11 (bottom background) LOC [LC-DIG-pga-01843], (bottom right) Appomattox Court House National Historical Park, National Park Service; p. 12 (right) LOC [LC-DIG-pga-07967], (left) LOC [LC-USZ62-72801]; p. 14 LOC [LC-USZC4-1526]; p. 15 MPI/Getty Images; p. 16 (left) LOC [LC-DIG-pga-00584], (center) LOC [LC-DIG-cwpb-04326]; p. 17 (bottom) LOC [LC-DIG-pga-01844]; p. 18 LOC [LC-USZ62-4063]; p. 19 (top) LOC [LC-DIG-pga-04033], (middle) Smithsonian Neg. No. 91-10712; Harpers Ferry NHP Cat. No. 13645, (bottom) Mike Cumpston/U.S. Wikipedia; p. 20 Ed Vebell/Getty Images; p. 21 The Abraham Lincoln Papers at the Library of Congress, Manuscript Division (Washington, D. C.: American Memory Project, [2000-02]); p. 22 LOC [LC-USZ62-17254]; p. 23 (top) LOC [LC-USZC2-1963], (bottom) LOC [LC-DIG-pga-07645]; p. 24 LOC [LC-DIG-highsm-04756]; p. 25 (bottom) LOC [LC-DIG-ppmsca-35137]; p. 27 (top) Andrew Russell/Buyenlarge/Getty Images; pp. 26-27 Universal History Archive/UIG via Getty images; pp. 27, 32 (middle) LOC [LC-DIG-ppmsca-33070]; p. 28 (left) LOC [LC-DIG-ds-07662]; p. 29 LOC [LC-DIG-cwpb-04326]; p. 31 LOC [LC-DIG-pga-00584]; back cover LOC [LC-USZC4-1526]; all other images from iStock and/or Shutterstock.

Library of Congress Cataloging-in-Publication Data

Names: Schwartz, Heather E., author.
Title: Causes of the Civil War : a house divided / Heather E. Schwartz.
Description: Huntington Beach, CA : Teacher Created Materials, Inc., 2017. | Includes index.
Identifiers: LCCN 2016034158 (print) | LCCN 2016040662 (ebook) | ISBN 9781493838035 (pbk.) | ISBN 9781480757684 (eBook)
Subjects: LCSH: United States--History--Civil War, 1861-1865--Causes--Juvenile literature. | Slavery--Southern States--History--Juvenile literature. | United States--Politics and government--1849-1861--Juvenile literature.
Classification: LCC E459 .S25 2017 (print) | LCC E459 (ebook) | DDC 973.7/11--dc23
LC record available at https://lccn.loc.gov/2016034158

Teacher Created Materials
5301 Oceanus Drive
Huntington Beach, CA 92649-1030
http://www.tcmpub.com

ISBN 978-1-4938-3804-2

Printed by 51250
PO 16654 / Printed in USA

Table of Contents

A Nation Divided

It's 1862. A soldier writes home to his wife. "It is rather bad to think that we should be fighting him on the one side and me on the other…I hope to god that he and I will get safe through it all and he will have his story to tell about his side and I will have my story to tell about my side."

The soldier's name is Alexander Campbell. He is a **Union** soldier fighting for the North. His brother, James, is a **Confederate** soldier fighting for the South. Without knowing it at the time, the two had recently fought each other on a battlefield during the Civil War.

The Civil War split the country apart. It divided families, friends, and countrymen. Americans were now fighting against each other. The North wanted to keep the country together. It was also fighting to end slavery. The South wanted to have its own nation. It wanted each state to decide about slavery on its own. Tensions built until war erupted. The two sides fought for four long years.

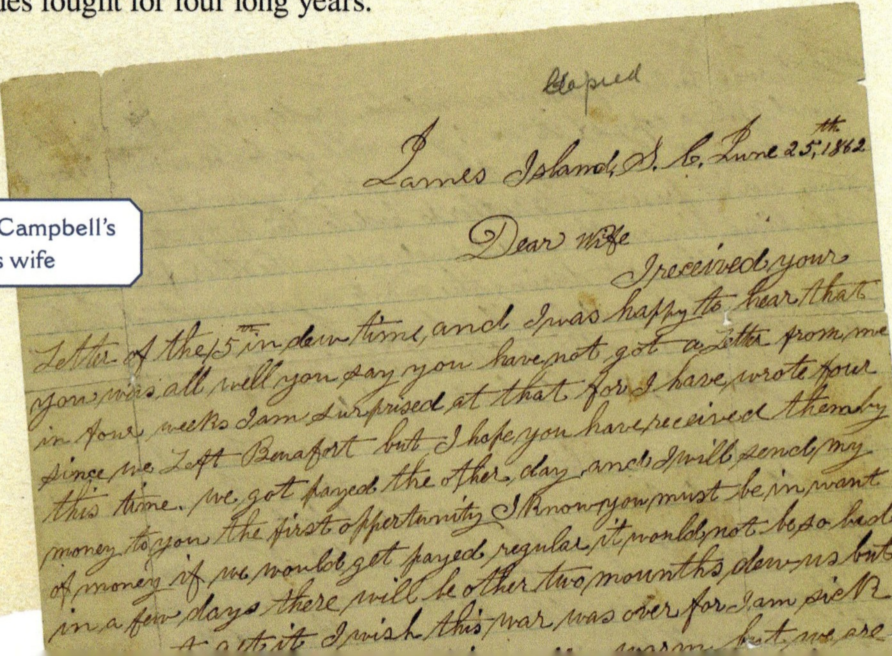

Copied

James Island, S. C. June 25th 1862

Dear Wife

I received your Letter of the 5th in dew time, and I was happy to hear that you was all well you say you have not got a Letter from me in four weeks I am surprised at that for I have wrote four since we Left Beaufort but I hope you have received them by this time. we got payed the other day and I will send my money to you the first opportunity I know you must be in want of money if we would get payed regular it would not be so bad in a few days there will be other two mounths dew us but … I wish this war was over for I am sick … warm but we are

Alexander Campbell's letter to his wife

The Campbell brothers fought each other during the Battle of Secessionville in 1862.

THE OUTCOME

The Campbell brothers survived the war. Both men went on to become successful American citizens. James owned a farm. Alexander had his own manufacturing business. The brothers remained friends throughout their lives.

James Campbell

Before the War

Years before the war began, the nation was drifting apart. People were fighting over two main issues—slavery and states' rights.

The South was mostly made up of farms. Southern farmers enslaved people to work without pay. As a result, the farmers made large **profits**. Some became very rich. The economy of the South relied on slavery. The South wanted to claim more land in the West. And it wanted slave labor to be allowed in this new land.

Enslaved people harvest sugarcane in the South.

FREE STATE
CONVENTION!

All persons who are favorable to a union of effort, and a permanent organization of all the Free State elements of Kansas Territory, and who wish to secure upon the broadest platform the co-operation of all who agree upon this point, are requested to meet at their several places of holding elections, in their respective districts on the 25th of August, instant, at one o'clock, P. M., and appoint five delegates to each representative to which they were entitled in the Legislative Assembly, who shall meet in general Convention at

Big Springs, Wednesday, Sept. 5th '55,

at 10 o'clock A. M., for the purpose of adopting a Platform upon which all may act harmoniously who prefer Freedom to Slavery.
The nomination of a Delegate to Congress, will also come up before the General Convention.
Let no sectional or party issues distract or prevent the perfect co-operation of Free State men. Union and harmony are absolutely necessary to success. The pro-slavery party are fully and effectually organized. No jars nor minor issues divide them. And to contend against them successfully, we also must be united— Without prudence and harmony of action we are certain to fail. Let every man then do his duty and we are certain of victory.
All Free State men, without distinction, are earnestly requested to take immediate and effective steps to insure a full and correct representation for every District in the Territory. "United we stand; divided we fall."
By order of the Executive Committee of the Free State Party of the Territory of Kansas, as per resolution of the Mass Convention in session at Lawrence, Aug 15th and 16th, 1855.

C. ROBINSON, Chairman.

J. K. GOODIN, Sec'y.

Herald of Freedom, Print.

an 1855 broadside advertising a convention to address the issue of slavery

The North didn't have as many farms. Instead, the people produced many types of goods and did not rely on slave labor. Many people in the North viewed slavery as **immoral**. It went against the Declaration of Independence, which states, "All men are created equal." Some Northerners wanted to stop the spread of slavery. They did not want it to be allowed in the new lands in the West. Others wanted to bring an end to slavery nationwide. They were called **abolitionists**. All this debate about slavery made the South feel threatened.

CHILD LABOR

The North may not have allowed slavery, but it had another form of cheap labor. Children often worked long hours in factories. Child laborers frequently worked in unsafe conditions for very little pay in order to earn money for their families.

Young boys work at a coal mine in the North.

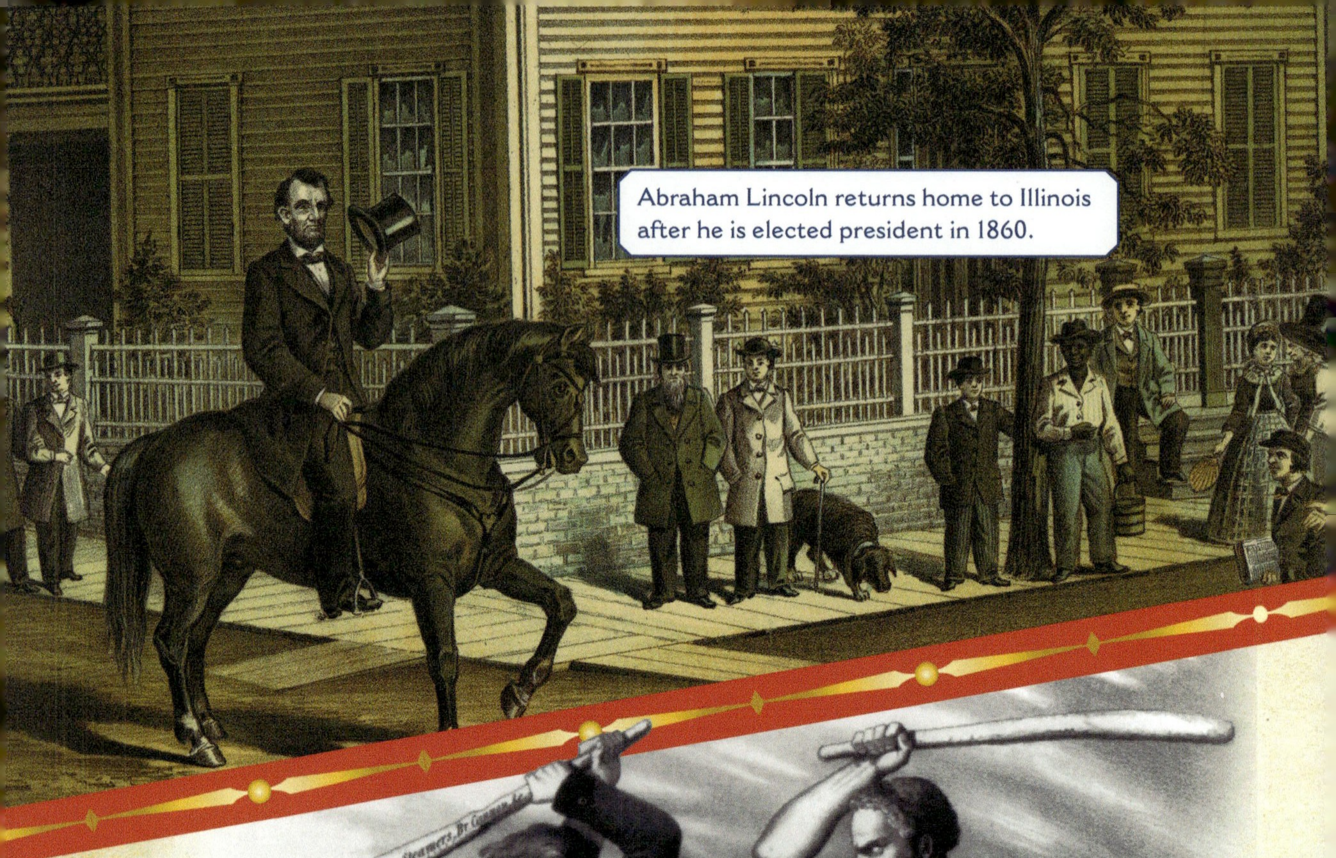

Abraham Lincoln returns home to Illinois after he is elected president in 1860.

This 1864 political cartoon shows the Union fighting against secession.

The South felt that the federal government should not have a say in the debate over slavery. It thought that each state government should decide. The North felt otherwise. It said it was not up to the states. The North called for the federal government to settle the dispute.

Tensions mounted as the North and the South grew further apart. In 1860, Abraham Lincoln was elected president. He was known for wanting to stop the spread of slavery. Lincoln taking office was the breaking point for the South. Southern states started to leave the Union. They formed the Confederacy.

Lincoln had stated that he would allow slavery in the South. He believed this would help keep the nation together. But, he did not want it to spread into the new territories. He hoped that slavery would die out over time. But one thing Lincoln would not tolerate was the country splitting in two. He wanted to keep the Union together. When the South **seceded**, Lincoln knew war was coming.

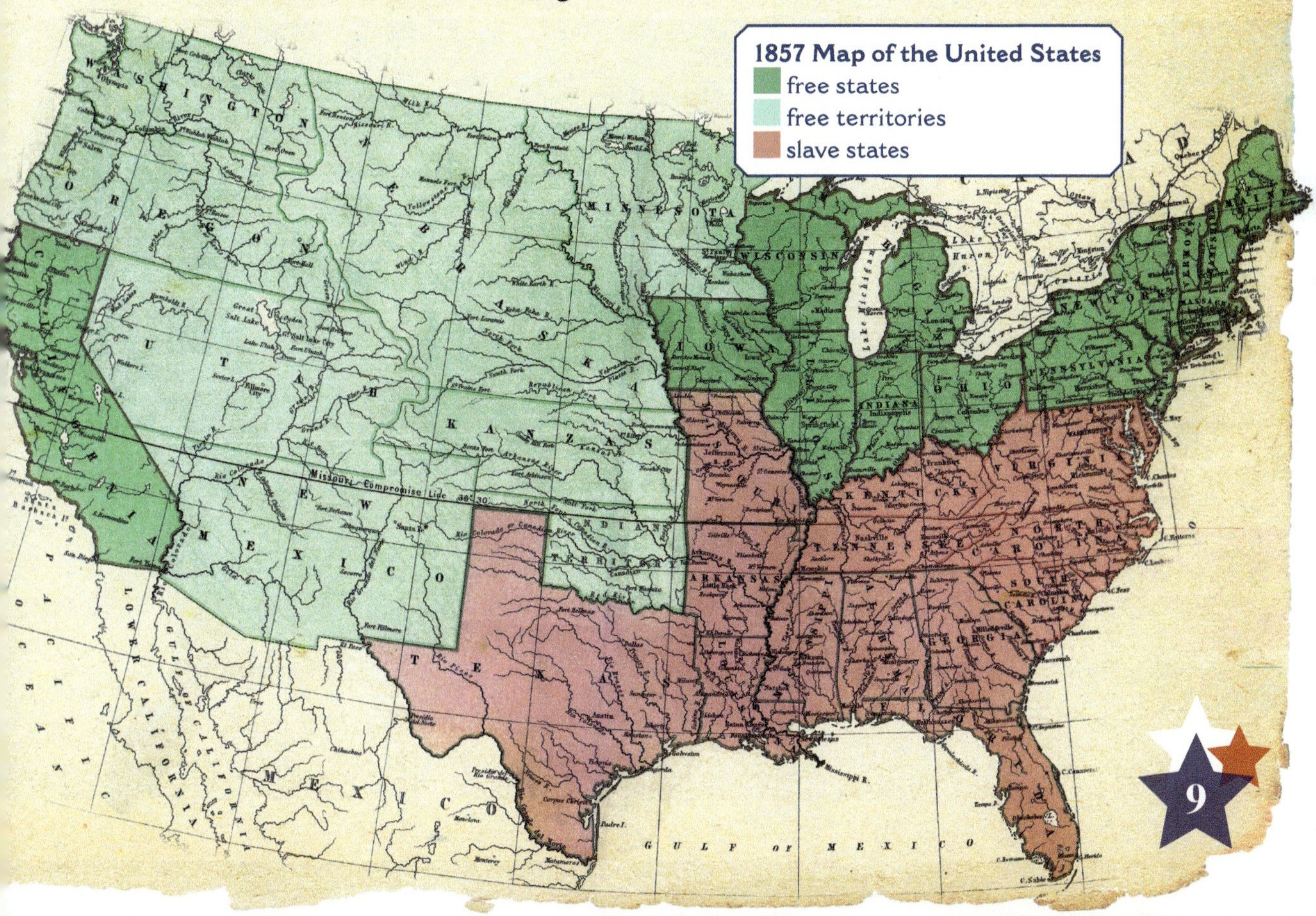

1857 Map of the United States
- free states
- free territories
- slave states

Battles Begin

Fort Sumter sat on an island off the South Carolina coast. Union troops stationed themselves there once the South seceded. Since the fort was in the South, Northerners were no longer welcome there. Southern troops sent ships to attack the fort. The first shots of the Civil War were fired at Fort Sumter on April 12, 1861. The fighting lasted 34 hours before Northern troops raised a white flag in **surrender**. The only death was a Confederate horse. The Civil War had begun.

WAVE THE FLAG

People were chosen to wave flags in battle. This showed where troops were and that they were still fighting. When the white flag replaced the Union flag at Fort Sumter, it was a sign of surrender.

Bull Run

Irvin McDowell

Stonewall Jackson

The first major battle of the Civil War was the First Battle of Bull Run. After the loss at Fort Sumter, Union troops marched to northern Virginia. General Irvin McDowell wanted to take over the Southern capital. On July 21, 1861, his troops ran into the Confederate army at a small creek called Bull Run. They began to fight.

One of the Confederate leaders was a man named Thomas Jackson. He helped his men stop the Union forces. One story says that his troops were like a wall the Union could not pass. Another claims that Jackson bravely fought the enemy with the resolve of a stone wall. Either way, Jackson inspired his men to fight. The South won the battle. And Jackson earned the nickname Stonewall Jackson.

THE UNFORTUNATE MR. MCLEAN

Wilmer McLean had a farm near Bull Run. One night, a cannonball smashed through his home. Three days later, the First Battle of Bull Run began. Confederate forces used his home as a headquarters, military hospital, and jail. So, McLean moved south to a town called Appomattox Court House. It would prove to be a fateful move.

the First Battle of Bull Run

Shiloh

The Union learned a lesson from the First Battle of Bull Run. It learned how strong the Confederate army was. Over the next year, more battles took place. The two armies clashed again and again.

In Tennessee, the Battle of Shiloh began on April 6, 1862. It was early in the morning. Union soldiers were eating breakfast. They received word that Confederate soldiers were heading straight for them. It was a surprise attack! Union soldiers scrambled to prepare for battle, but they did not have enough time. In just two hours, they heard an eerie rebel yell. The enemy was upon them.

Bullets filled the air. As they whizzed past, soldiers thought they sounded like hornets. The site of the battle later became known as the Hornet's Nest. The fight lasted all day. That night, the South claimed the battle as a victory. But, the fighting was not over. More Union soldiers arrived overnight. The next morning, Grant ordered a **counterattack**. Union troops forced the Confederates to **retreat**. The fighting ceased. More than 23,000 Americans lay dead.

General Sherman's men were attacked at the Battle of Shiloh.

Ulysses S. Grant

Battle of Shiloh

WOMEN AND THE WAR

While men fought, women did many jobs normally done by men. They farmed and worked in factories. Some raised money for the armies by selling homemade goods. Others went to the front lines as nurses and spies. Some even dressed as men and fought!

The War Moves North

By the fall of 1862, the South had won numerous battles. Robert E. Lee was proving to be one of the greatest generals in the war. Lee devised a plan to march his troops into the North. He knew there would be more crops and supplies there. The South had been running low on resources. The war had devastated their supplies.

Lee led his troops into Maryland. This was the first time the South marched its troops into the North. Luckily for the North, a Union soldier found a pack of cigars. The paper the cigars were wrapped in had Lee's plan of attack written on it. The North now knew where Lee's troops were going and what Lee was planning to do.

Lincoln meets with McClellan at Antietam.

THE EMANCIPATION PROCLAMATION

After Antietam, Lincoln issued the Emancipation Proclamation. It ended slavery in the South, but not in the border states or the Southern states already controlled by the North. It also let African Americans join the Union army. Many joined and fought bravely.

General McClellan at Antietam

The fighting began on September 17 at Antietam Creek. There was so much fog and smoke in the air that soldiers could barely see. The fighting lasted 12 hours. Union troops had chances to win, but General George McClellan did not send in **reserve** troops. He was too cautious. The Union won in the end, but the **casualties** were enormous.

Battle of Antietam

Leaders in the War

There were many other key battles in the Civil War that proved to be fierce and pivotal. Soldiers on both sides fought passionately for their cause. In the end, it was leadership that made the difference. The great leaders of the Civil War are remembered to this day. They gave everything they had to the war effort. They worked hard. They inspired those fighting on the battlefields. Three of the main leaders were General Robert E. Lee, President Lincoln, and General Ulysses S. Grant. They played important roles in the Civil War. These are some of their memorable moments.

the Battle of Chancellorsville

Lee's Greatest Victory

In the spring of 1863, General Lee displayed great military skill. He planned a genius defensive move during the Battle of Chancellorsville. This was in the wilderness of Virginia.

The Union had Lee's army surrounded and outnumbered. But, Lee had a plan. He split his army in two! He sent General "Stonewall" Jackson and his men to surprise the Union troops. The **flank** attack was a success. The battle raged on for days. But now, the Union was on the defensive. Lee once again split his army. On May 6, he won the battle. Next, he marched north to Gettysburg.

Lee visits Jackson's grave.

LEE'S GREATEST LOSS

One night during the Battle of Chancellorsville, Jackson went scouting. He was badly wounded by his own troops. They had mistaken him for the enemy. Jackson died a few days later of pneumonia (nuh-MOH-nyuh), caused by an infection. His death left Lee with a strong sense of grief and loss.

Lincoln Addresses the Nation

President Lincoln is the most well-known leader from the Civil War. His job was filled with stress. He had to make many hard decisions. But his resolve made him a strong leader. His wise ways helped hold a nation together. One of his finest moments during the war came after the Battle of Gettysburg.

The Battle of Gettysburg was the deadliest of all Civil War battles. It took place in a small town in Pennsylvania. It began on July 1, 1863. A group of soldiers from the North and the South began firing at each other. The next day, more soldiers from both sides arrived. The Union troops took the high ground. Lee saw them and ordered his troops to charge up the hill and attack. By the end of the day, thousands of soldiers from both sides lay dead.

On July 3, Lee sent his men across a mile of flat land. Because the Union army was high off the ground, it had no problem attacking Southern troops. Later that night, Lee's army retreated. The whole battle lasted three days. As many as 51,000 men were injured, captured, or killed.

Abraham Lincoln

Battle of Gettysburg

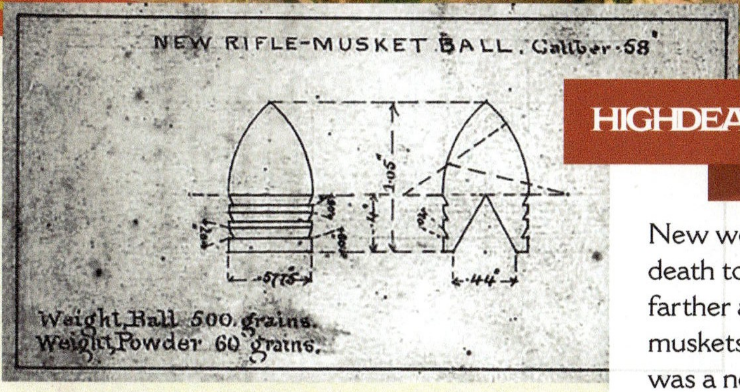

HIGH DEATH TOLLS

New weapons increased the death toll in the war. Rifles shot farther and more accurately than muskets. The Minié (MINI) ball was a new type of bullet. They were easy to load. Repeating rifles fired more than one bullet before being reloaded.

When the battle ended, the dead were buried where they fell. People wanted to honor those who lost their lives at Gettysburg. By the end of the year, Gettysburg had become a national cemetery. President Lincoln was asked to speak at the **dedication**. On November 19, 1863, Lincoln rose and addressed the crowd. He spoke for just two minutes, but the speech was moving. Today, we know it as the Gettysburg Address.

Lincoln delivers the Gettysburg Address.

Lincoln reminded the crowd why the war was being fought. He quoted the Declaration of Independence. He said that the nation was founded on the belief that "all men are created equal." And yet, there were people who were not free. He said it was important to fight for their freedom. It was important to fight for American values. By saving the Union, they were saving **democracy**. They would show the world that a country based on freedom could succeed. It could survive.

Lincoln's leadership during the war would endear him to the nation. He would go down in history as one of the most beloved presidents.

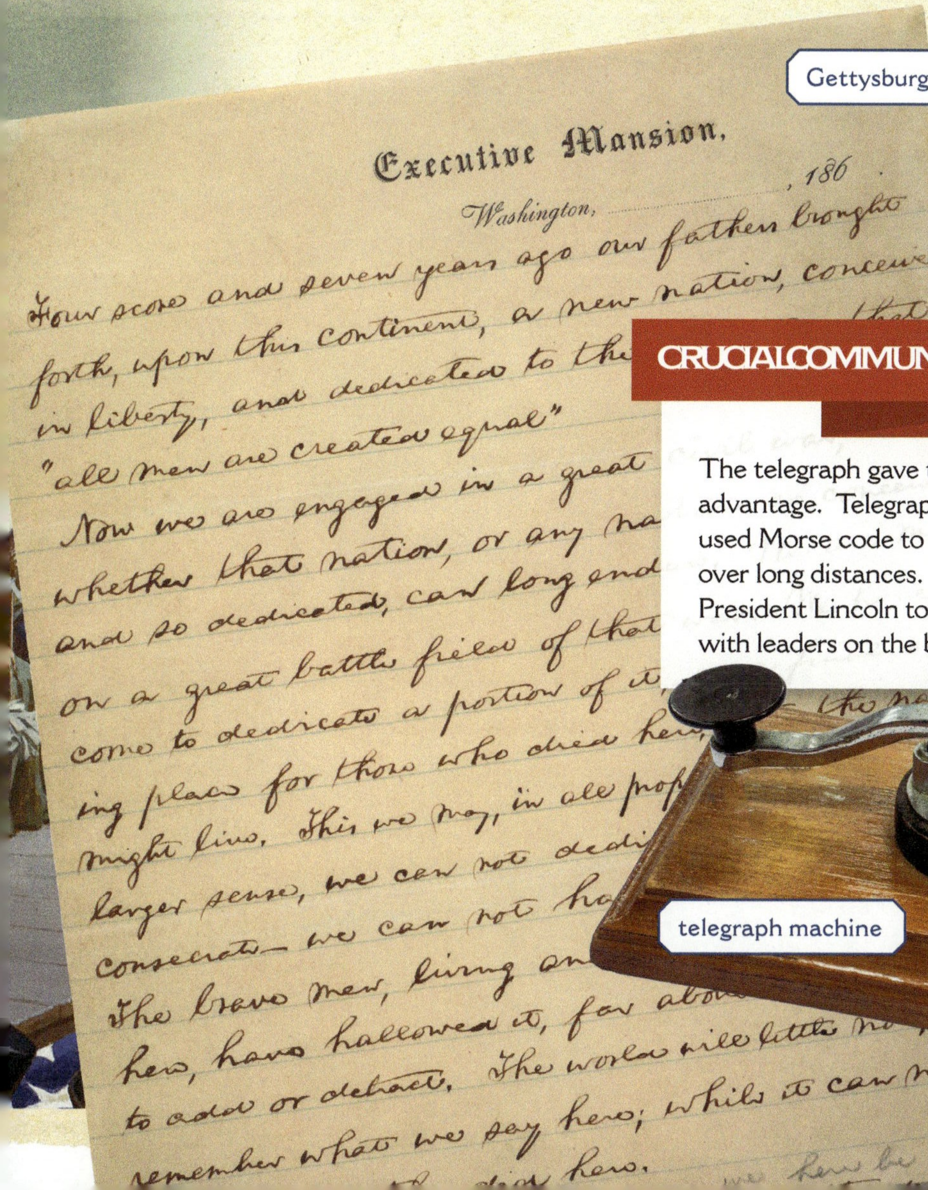
Executive Mansion,

Washington, , 186

Four score and seven years ago our fathers brought forth, upon this continent, a new nation, conceived in liberty, and dedicated to the

"all men are created equal"

Now we are engaged in a great

whether that nation, or any

and so dedicated, can long

on a great battle field of that

come to dedicate a portion of it,

ing place for those who died here,

might live. This we may, in all

larger sense, we can not

consecrate we can not

The brave men, living and

here, have hallowed it, far above

to add or detract. The world will little

remember what we say here; while it can never

Gettysburg Address

CRUCIAL COMMUNICATIONS

The telegraph gave the North a huge advantage. Telegraph operators used Morse code to send messages over long distances. This allowed President Lincoln to communicate with leaders on the battlefield.

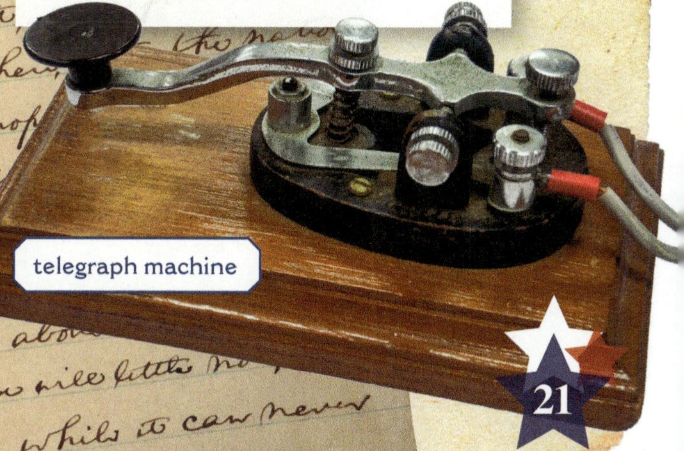
telegraph machine

Grant Gains Power

President Lincoln admired Ulysses S. Grant. He respected the way he fought the war. He was forceful. He did not give up. In the last two years of the war, Grant gained key victories for the Union.

One of Grant's greatest victories came in 1863. The city of Vicksburg overlooked the Mississippi River. Whichever side controlled Vicksburg also controlled the river. Grant marched his men toward the city. But he could not find a way to break through the rebel forces. So, he blocked the city from receiving any outside supplies. This is called a **siege**. Soon, Confederate soldiers began to starve. On July 4, 1863, they surrendered. This was a huge win for Grant.

RAILWAYS AND THE WAR

The North and South both used railroads to transport supplies. But the North had an advantage. It had more tracks and only used one type of car. The railroads in the South were different widths. So, they had to use different cars on different tracks. Also, the trains in the South ran much slower than those in the North.

Petersburg, Virginia, 1865

In June 1864, the fighting moved to Petersburg, Virginia. General Grant heard about a large railway system there. Grant also knew that Lee was there with his men. Grant thought that if he could defeat Lee's army and take control of the railway, the war would end. The Confederate army was far outnumbered. After almost a year of fighting, Lee and his men moved out of the area. Lee felt that his army was falling apart. Grant thought an end to the war was near.

Ulysses S. Grant

The South Surrenders

On April 9, 1865, General Lee's men were fighting Union troops in a town called Appomattox Court House. General Lee was watching the battle. He thought his men were winning. But then, more Union troops showed up to help. Lee's men were outnumbered. They were weak and tired. They had no food and were hungry. Lee decided it was time to surrender. General Lee ordered white flags to be raised over the battlefield. He sent a note to General Grant asking to meet with him that afternoon.

The two men met in the **parlor** of a local house. Lee officially surrendered to Grant. Grant told Lee that his soldiers could return to their homes. But first, they must hand over any horses and weapons that were owned by the army. All Union prisoners of war were to be released, as well. Grant could have demanded much more. But he wanted to unite the country again.

Battles continued until word of Lee's surrender spread to all troops. The last shots of the war were fired on May 13, 1865. The final surrender was signed on June 2. Over time, the Southern states that had seceded were allowed back into the Union. The war was over.

War Department, Washington, April 20, 1865.
$100,000 REWARD
THE MURDERER
Of our late beloved President, ABRAHAM LINCOLN,
IS STILL AT LARGE.
0,000 REWARD
by this Department for his apprehension, in addition to any reward offered by Municipal Authorities or State Executives.
,000 REWARD!
be paid for the apprehension of JOHN H. SURRATT, one of Booth's accomplices.
$25,000 REWARD!
will be paid for the apprehension of DANIEL C. HARROLD, another of Booth's accomplices.

THE DEATH OF A PRESIDENT

Five days after Lee's surrender, an angry Southerner named John Wilkes Booth killed President Lincoln. While Lincoln was watching a play, Booth sneaked into the president's private box and shot him. Lincoln died the following morning.

Lee surrenders to Grant.

THE UNFORTUNATE MR. MCLEAN, PART II

The home where Lee and Grant met just happened to belong to Wilmer McLean—the same man whose farm was taken over at Bull Run. Many say the war started and ended with Mr. McLean.

McLean's home in Appomattox Court House, Virginia

Reunite, Rebuild, and Recover

Towns had been burned to the ground. Fields that were once full of crops were now covered with the bodies of dead soldiers. Churches and homes had been transformed into makeshift hospitals. Families were left without fathers and brothers. The effects of this war would be felt for many years to come.

Slavery was fully **abolished** a few months after the war ended. But, racism was not. African Americans now had to adjust to a new way of living. They were free and independent. Yet, they faced prejudice at every turn. Many people continued to see them as if they were less than human. Some still treated them as slaves.

SURPRISING STATISTICS

- An average of 504 soldiers died per day.
- Three out of every five Union soldiers and two out of every three Confederate soldiers died from disease rather than in battle.
- One in ten Union soldiers were African Americans.
- One in three Union soldiers were immigrants.
- About 40 percent of dead soldiers were never identified.

Civil War hospital

destroyed railroad in Virginia

It would take time to rebuild and reunite the nation. The war was one of the costliest wars in American history. It was costly because of the destruction. It was costly because of the casualties. But, it was also costly because it was a war fought on American soil. It was a war fought between Americans. It truly was a war in which brother fought against brother. Recovering from the war was a long and difficult process.

ruins of a street in Richmond, Virginia

Publish It!

Pretend you are a newspaper publisher. Pick a day during the Civil War. It could be the day the war started or the day it ended. It could be a day an important battle or event took place. Think about the details of that day. Then, create the front page of a newspaper describing it. Your newspaper page should have a title, a big headline, pictures, an advertisement related to the war, the date, and at least one story. Once you have created it, publish it! Make copies to share with friends and family.

FRANK LESLIE'S ILLUSTRATED NEWSPAPER

No. 446—Vol. XVIII.] NEW YORK, MAY 7, 1864.

HARPER'S WEEKLY. A JOURNAL OF CIVILIZATION

Vol. VIII.—No. 392.] NEW YORK, SATURDAY, JULY 2, 1864.

GEN. ROBERT EDMUND LEE.

THE REBEL GENERAL ROBERT EDMUND LEE.

President Lincoln and other leaders at Antietam

Glossary

abolished—to have officially ended or stopped something

abolitionists—people who were against slavery and worked to end it

casualties—people who are hurt or killed during an accident or war

Confederate— belonging to the group of Southern states that seceded from the United States during the Civil War

counterattack—to attack after having already defended a position

dedication—a ceremony to name or set aside somewhere for a special purpose

democracy—a form of government in which people choose their leaders by voting in elections

flank—the right or left side of a military formation

immoral—wrong or evil; not good

parlor—a room in a house that is used for spending time and communicating with guests

profits—money that is made in a business after all of the costs have been paid

reserve—extra soldiers waiting to fight

retreat—a military strategy that involves pulling back or leaving a battle

seceded—formally separated from a nation or state

siege—a military blockade of an area that cuts off all contact with the outside world

surrender—an agreement to stop fighting because victory is unattainable

Union—belonging to the Northern army during the Civil War

Index

Your Turn!

The South in Ruins

This photo was taken in 1865 in Richmond, Virginia. Many Southern cities like this one were destroyed. It took years for the South to recover from the Civil War. How would you describe this photo? What do you imagine the people in the photo are thinking? How does this photo show the effects of the Civil War on the South? Write a paragraph to answer these questions.